How We Sleep on the Nights We Don't Make Love

poems by
E. Ethelbert Miller

CURBSTONE PRESS

The poems in this book have been previously published in the following journals: *5AM, Howard Magazine, Washington Review, Tight, Margie, Blue Fifth Review,* and *Blackbird Magazine;* and in the anthology: *Identity Lessons: Contemporary Writing About Learning to Be American,* edited by Maria Mazziotti Gillan and Jennifer Gillan.

Printed in Canada on acid-free paper by Transcontinental / Best Book
Cover design: Stone Graphics
Cover art: "Okomfo, the Musician-Magician" by Edgar H.
    Sorrells-Adewale; sand, acrylic paint; 1974.

 This book was published with the support of the Connecticut Commission on the Arts, the National Endowment for the Arts, and
NATIONAL ENDOWMENT FOR THE ARTS donations from many individuals. We are very grateful for all of their support.
Connecticut Commission on the Arts

Library of Congress Cataloging-in-Publication Data

Miller, E. Ethelbert.
    How we sleep on the nights we don't make love : poems / by E.
    Ethelbert Miller.— 1st ed.
        p. cm.
    ISBN 1-931896-04-6 (pbk. : alk. paper)
    I. Title.
        PS3563.I3768H69 2004
    811'.54—dc22   2003025009

published by
CURBSTONE PRESS   321 Jackson Street   Willimantic CT 06226
            phone: 860-423-5110   e-mail: info@curbstone.org
                            www.curbstone.org

Contents

Introduction

Poetry keeps E. Ethelbert Miller up. No, he has no trouble getting out of bed because he is awake all the time. Read this book. You'll see. He thinks of the world or of someone in the world nearly day and night, and his Buddhist teachings lead him to loving detachment. Yet, our interior and exterior lives require a common thread taut between them, and Ethelbert spins his own yarn by his continual attempts to understand and love those around him. If you know Ethelbert, you know how often he pats you on the back, holds your hand, rubs your head (or even your ear, for that matter); if you do not know Ethelbert, his poems will do it for him.

Miller, who calls himself one of the original Bronx Bombers and who puts the onus of the Boston Red Sox's Bambino Curse not on the sale of Babe Ruth but on management's treatment of its first black player Pumpsie Green, is one of the hardest workingmen in the book business. Poet, memoirist, anthologist, editor, activist, TV show host, radio personality, Director of the African American Resource Center at Howard University since 1974, Miller is one of the founders of the Humanities Council in Washington, DC. His list of posts from Commissioner of the DC Commission on the Arts and Humanities to core faculty member at Bennington College's Writing Seminars only nominally explain all he does for literature. Never has there been a writer more generous with his time for those willing to put in the work and apt to submit him or herself to the grind necessary to get to nonexistent there.

Read Ethelbert Miller's poems as if he is sitting next to you telling you things in a low voice so that no one else can hear him. Miller's playfulness runs throughout his poems and his life. If he is near, you will first hear his laugh as he cajoles while never losing sight of the social context of the moment. In Vermont once, he waved to a friend, who could not from afar recognize him. "What? You can't recognize me—the only black man in this state?" he laughingly called out.

Miller's poems side with hope, love, and humanity. Despite his calls for prayer, Miller avoids metaphysics; he is a love poet among natural objects—a wet towel, a tube of toothpaste, a comb, a bathroom faucet, a bridge, a hat, a steering wheel, and some lost keys. Like the poet, his muses also do not relent. All nine sisters put in their time. The reader will find epic topics, historical allusions, musical references, love poems, Katherine Dunham and dance, tragic conse-quences of human behavior, life's comedies, songs of Bird, and even astronomical observations.

On the front page of our newspapers, we read daily of the Middle East struggle. Many American poets do not touch this subject matter. Nope, the personal innocuous subjective fills their pages from front to back. However, in *How We Sleep on the Nights We Don't Make Love*, Ethelbert connects the Palestinian situation to the treatment of African-Americans before the U.S. civil rights movement. In his poem 'Rosa Parks dreams' Ms. Parks dreams of sitting in the charred chassis of a Levantine bombed-out bus—the horrific sight so great even the roadside wildflowers stare back in shock. Miller's poems do what poems should do—compress and raise understanding. His poems dealing with the Middle East struggle do not side with either team. Though he sees the injustices made against Palestinians, he acknowledges their violent acts, too. This furious City of God only has humans living among the debris. We all live there, as does Omar, who you will meet in the following pages. To choose the only team fighting in the street—the human race—demands great courage of him: Miller believes with full faith in the transformative powers of love and understanding.

To have such understanding, Miller must be able to listen and have that sense of humor. He and I have discussed at length the struggles for American poets in the face of our society's overweening materialism. He once wrote to me, "I prefer to have someone reading one of my poems long after I'm gone...and getting a nice feeling in their heart. I don't need the car...I can't drive. I have the house...is this heaven?"

Nope. Boundaries fade away as people raise them repeatedly day after day. The difficulty lies in trying to keep together all the daily fragments we make. With a rare humanity to embrace our beauty and horror, Ethelbert Miller has found a way.

—Anastasios Kozaitis

to
Zoe Anglesey
Reetika Vazirani

How We Sleep on the Nights
We Don't Make Love

Salat

poetry is prayer
light dancing inside words

five times a day
I try to write

step by step
I move towards the mihrab

I prepare to recite
what is in my heart

I recite your name

Untitled

I've been
kissing
your eyes
too long

haven't
your
lips
noticed?

Morning Raga

(for Meera)

your beauty
is one whole
note

I watch
the sun
rise in
the
center
of your
brow

4/20/88

Hi J
I decided to rewrite what I sent to you
(for June Jordan)

our friendship
is what keeps us whole
love is essential as air

prayer contains desire
to worship is to open
the door to one's heart

we were looking at
the ceiling and then
we saw the sky

10/24/98

May 26, 2002

The Lakers won tonight because
Robert Horry hit a three pointer
at the buzzer. I miss you.
I'm always touching your rim
and slipping out. Maybe it's my
east coast style or John Coltrane
playing "Too Young To Go Steady"
on his Ballads album. Sometimes
the music bounces like a ball and
love is something you can't catch
so you keep shooting.

5/27/02

A Portrait in Nine Lines

I want to hold your face in my hands
just for its laughter. I love your hat.
I was standing in a bookstore when
you turned the corner. Page after page
reminds me of your arms. The wind
sits in a park reading a book of your
poems. Is today your birthday? Yes
is such an easy word to say. I know.
This is the portrait of you I love.

A Portrait of Yes in Fourteen Lines

I want to hold your face in my hands
and share my laughter with your eyes.
I love your hat. I can see your hair
giving my heart directions again. I was
standing in a bookstore across town
when I turned and found
my way to the poetry section. I like
how poem after poem reminds me of
your arms. I once sat in a park
reading about birds. I was hungry for
love. I cried when the crumbs were
gone. I thought today was your birthday.
I had a present for you. I know this poem
will say yes to everything you do.

Kiss

three times I wanted
to kiss you

place my hand
on your breast

the tip of your nipple
finding my palm

and wearing it
like a hat

what should my
other hand wear?

my fingers so wet
from your rain

Bridge

we breathe

and walk and talk
and the bridge
is between us

and beneath us

and we are the
bridge and no
one walks

below

What Does the E Stand For?

Everything
Each eye exists embracing exceptional emerald evenings
Evolution explains Eden's evil
Earth's ecology equates exploitation evaporation
Errors ending evergreen elms
Escort elephants eagles elks eastward
Enlightenment echoes Ezra Ezekiel
Enlist Esther Eugene Ethan Edward Ellington
Enough English explanations ecco
Exit eternity
Elucidate Ethelbert elucidate
E evokes every ecstatic emotion

1/21/02

Car Problems

I don't know how to drive.
All my problems begin with
cars. I am being driven crazy.
Could you take the wheel?
Is this a right turn or no parking
zone? Buckle up. I like your
headlights. Do you need a ride?
My meter just expired. Do you
have any change? What color
is your car? Do you want to
sit in the front or back? I always
walk, always go, never stop.
This poem is turning green.

Toothpaste

after dinner
you have the habit
of curling up in
the couch
like a tube of
toothpaste all bent
funny and nice
I like to brush
after every meal

Waves

I rise tall and dark
Your mouth is like an ocean
I watch the waves come

Honey

Your petals open
Sweet honey inside of you
My tongue licks the jar

Bloom

I return now to find you as beautiful as fresh cut
flowers placed in a window of a corner store on
a weekend when no one is around to notice

except me and I say hello to you

in bloom
my hands touching the glass between us and the
sun's sun

Waco, Texas

somewhere north
you rise from your bed
reaching
what else is there to hold?

The Seduction of Light

I place your slippers together and place them
in the corner. I make the bed. I touch the place
where you slept. There is only a trace of you.
A wet towel, a tube of toothpaste, a comb with
your hair—still wet. I stop and think of how little
we talk. I hear the dripping from the bathroom
faucet, the dog barking next door. Through the
curtains sunlight stretches and spreads herself
across the rug. So seductive is light whenever
she places a hand on a wall. I wait inside the
room curling against a picture like smoke. The
end of love is a photograph found in a wallet.
I reach into my pockets for my keys. I am leaving.
I slip my shoes on.

Diva

feathers on my arms
the way they caress like air
his hands only a memory
a ring sitting like an owl
on a bedroom dresser
I close my eyes
to the applause of tears

XandO

(for Naomi)

The world is going to work
as I sit in a café talking
with Naomi, a poet who dreams
in another language.

There are crumbs on
the table from our morning breakfast
and like periods they punctuate our
conversation.

Why do I mistake the loneliness
of a napkin for my heart?

Four Lines

I keep wanting to undress you
in 2 languages but I only know 1

I took your book to bed
I fell asleep with you in my mouth

Victoria Sitting In Usdan Gallery

A man could fall
in love with your eyes
but then what would
he see?

Across the room you
sit illuminated by
grace and beauty

Someone is reading
a poem. I hear
nothing until you
push your hair
away from your face

Las Cruces

(for Margo)

We are standing in the middle
of the road—talking for the
first time. The dust of our lives
coming together to create something
new. I look into your eyes and
see words falling from
a poem I cannot write. How can
anyone explain this moment? I want
to embrace you—hold your heart.
Do you hear the wind?

3/26/02

Memory Loss

I remember it like a page
turning

and something happening
for just a moment.

Your dress escaping
up your legs

and...

2/16/02

Drummers?

the heart
is a drum

but
who will teach us
to listen?

what sound
will it make?

love?

how deaf
we are

Space Is the Place

Love is the last planet in our solar
system. Your heart crying like the
rings of Saturn. How can we believe
in stars in this darkness? I watch
the sky for your return. Inside my
hands nothing but gravity.

See

Seeing you
is like seeing you
for the first time
and wanting to
see you again.

How many men
have said they
loved you only
to say it again
and again?

I love you
I said it again

see.

Rosa Parks dreams

Rosa Parks dreams about
a bus in Jerusalem. A headless
woman sits in her seat. There is no
driver today. The top of the bus
is missing. On the road a line
of bodies segregated from the living.
They sleep against a twisted metal
frame. Wild flowers stare from
a field.

Honey & Watermelons

A man is making a bomb.
His slender fingers
are like threads and wires
weaving into metal.

The man is not thinking
of destruction or how a
child might lose a limb
or a mother a child.

He is thinking of honey
and watermelons and a
countless number of virgins
to hold his hands.

The man is thinking of
paradise and how this life
is an illusion and what
he is making is not a bomb.

On the table next to his
tools is a book filled
with wonder and miracles
he cannot understand.

The man is hungry for
the next life so he
completes his work
and cleans his table.

A man is walking down
the street with a bomb.
He stops next to a man
who looks like me.

Speechless in September

It was the first day of science fiction
so I expected a second moon or sun to appear.

Those of us who claimed to be people of the book
wept after the destruction of Borders bookstore.

Vendors sold masks and bottled water to strangers
who walked out of the dust holding cell phones and palm pilots.

I took this to be an omen of things to come,
the answer to the great riddles of our time:

Why do they hate us?
Who let the dogs out?

Nails

When my body divided itself into parts
I didn't see my entire life flash before my eyes.
I was distracted by nails biting my bones
hammering my head into pavement.

One hand was turned into a glove of blood
the other was already missing.

I saw myself as a small child in Brooklyn
ashamed to tell my mother that the money
stuffed inside my glove was gone.

In the kitchen I stood by the hot stove
crying and wishing there was somewhere to hide.

A young man walks through the doorway
of a café and proclaims himself a magician.
He is a Palestinian whose land has disappeared.

Where is his mother?

What will he see before he dies?
How many other young men are busy
counting the fingers on their hands,

waiting to escape into paradise
nails exploding in their hearts?

A Middle Class Algerian Woman
in Paris Talks about Fashion

Another day of headlines from Algeria.
I comb my hair while thinking about the news from home.
Small children and women are having their throats cut,
and my nails need to be painted.
What color dress should I wear? Is black too formal?
Of course I'll cover my head.
I can't afford another trip to the beauty parlor.
It's either sunglasses or a veil.
So what does the Quran say today?
Should I stay in Paris or go to Algiers?
It's always a question of money or murder.
I don't know anything about politics.
I think the soldiers are cute but too much into guns.

1/13/98

31

Throwing Stones at the Porno Star

It was I who threw the first stone
at her head. I said a prayer to Allah
asking for forgiveness. For a moment
I wanted to see her body. I wanted to
see sin close-up. In the prison courtyard
she was buried with only her head exposed
and naked like a breast. I threw a second
and third stone. I turned to find a fourth.
Even when her eyes closed and her blood
flowed like piss, I did not stop. How could
I? Is this not the blessing of believers?

Song for an Angel

(for S.H.)

Middle Eastern blues
tonight and I wonder why
you live in Brooklyn

and not somewhere in my
heart or right inside a kiss
outside from everything

that's wrong with the world

Malik

Malik mumbled Arabic
over his plate like someone
adding salt before tasting.
Islam had been good to him.
It was light slipping
between prison bars,
changing shadows into prayer
rugs.

When Malik thought about the
murder he had committed
his hands tighten around his
Quran and Mecca seemed as
far away as freedom.

A few guards and prisoners
thought Malik's new faith
was a gimmick, a safety device
or a wall to protect one's back
from a punch.

Renee who called herself Malik's
girlfriend still wore short skirts
when she went to see him.
It was her way of slapping the face
of God for taking her man away.

Freedom Candy

So what kind of name is Omar?
I ask this new boy at school.
You named after a candy bar or what?
You know you too light to be milk chocolate

Omar looks at me and laughs.
Since that first smile he's my best friend,
maybe my best friend ever.

Folks call us the inseparables
like one of those old singing groups
my daddy is always talking about.

Omar is a muslim name Omar tells me.
I think it still sounds like a candy bar,
like O'Henry, Baby Ruth, Mars or Almond Joy.

Maybe his momma should have named him
Snickers because of the way he laughs.
Omar's name sounds like candy
and the way he acts is sweet to me.

Every teacher except Mrs. Greenfield thinks so.
Ms. Greenfield she don't like Muslims
and the rest of us she calls natural born sinners
because of the way we talk and behave.

Omar says we should tell Mrs. Greenfield
about herself since it's Black History Month.
So Omar stands up and says to Mrs. Greenfield:

How come you don't lead us somewhere?
Why you not like Harriet Tubman?
Why no field trips?
Why no trips to the museum or zoo?
Why we never go nowhere, why?

Mrs. Greenfield, she don't say nothing.
She just look at Omar as if he is the last Muslim
on earth and is about to die.

I think of how Omar says Muslims pray
five times a day and how cats have nine lives and
just maybe Omar might make it to 3 o'clock
or maybe he won't.

Suddenly Mrs. Greenfield has one of those
fainting spells just like old Moses Tubman.
She has to sit down behind her desk so
she tells me to go get her some water.

I feel free as I race down the hall
wondering how Omar can be sweet sometimes
and get on everyone's nerves the next.

My daddy once told me M&Ms
melt in your mouth and your hands
especially if you colored.

Wait until I tell Omar.

Sister Sheba, Omar & Me

Sister Sheba
She's my cousin
She lives across town
where my momma tells me not to go
not unless it's daytime
and the sun is out bright

Don't you go over there
without asking my momma say
and when I ask her she tells me *no*
so I don't ask no more
You know what I mean?

And so I have to wait for Sister Sheba
to come see me and tell me everything
my momma don't want me to know

So why you have a Muslim for a friend?
she asks me the next weekend my aunt visits
my momma and Sister Sheba visits me

Sister Sheba
she's always trying to get into your business
which is why she don't have no time for herself
Her hair be flying all different ways and my
momma don't even want to let her in the house
and if she see her outside she don't say she's
family because why embarrass yourself in public
if you don't have to
That's what my momma say
and that's what Anna Banana says too

Anna Banana is my guidance counselor
Her real name is Mrs. Bernstein
but everyone calls her Anna Banana
because she's always telling kids

that if they would give up
junk food and just eat fruits
and vegetables everything would be
OK in school

Our grades would improve and we would have
what she calls self esteem and be like white
kids which is crazy to me since we're all black
and that's why we call Mrs. Bernstein Anna
Banana and my momma calls her a real fruitcake
and says *that woman shouldn't even be around
kids let alone trying to guide them somewhere*
and today Sister Sheba
Sounds just like Anna Banana
asking why I have a Muslim for a friend

She saw Omar in my house last month
and asked me where his shoes were. I said
*They by the front door, didn't you see them
when you came in?*

Omar takes off his shoes
whenever he comes to see me
just like in the mosque he's always talking
about and I ain't seen because my momma
say *boy you was a problem in my womb and
so I don't need you around no strange influences*

So I don't get to go to the mosque with Omar
but he gets to play with me because momma say
That boy should have some fun
Most Muslims I see don't even smile she tells me

What the Lord give you teeth for
if you can't smile?

So I tell Sister Sheba
to get her face out of mine and leave Omar alone
and why she can't mind her own business when
she visits is beyond me

Omar says I should pray or do salat
Something like that because Sister Sheba
lives where the bad boys are

Omar says she's gonna have a baby and maybe
never finish school
I tell Omar to *Shhhhhhhhhh..and hush his face*
Sometimes Omar can be a real Anna Banana
but he still my best friend
My best friend ever or what my momma calls
an apple in the hands of Eve

Hmmm
I wonder what my momma means by that
You think Mrs. Bernstein knows?

Omar, Books and Me

Folks call Omar a bookhead and me a bookend.
I don't read too much because I don't have time.
I don't even wear a watch to remind myself.

Why should I look at lines
on a page if they don't move
like the movies?

Omar reads so much about black history
and black heroes, I tell him he's gonna
be left behind living in a pyramid or something.

Omar says he looks Egyptian and maybe I should
look in the mirror and find myself too.
He laughs at me and takes a swing at my head.

You gonna be a bookend forever with folks
pushing you out the way like you at the end
of the shelf of life.

I listen to Omar and shake my head.
The end of the shelf of life sounds
like one of those soap shows Natalie watches.

She's always crying about some fool in love.
Omar says Natalie is my other bookend
and maybe that's why I'm afraid of books.

I laugh and tell him Natalie is his girlfriend.
You read your face Omar.
Boy, you should read your face.

I run down the street with my sneakers untied,
tripping over myself and being silly.
Omar runs after me shouting about how he plans

to bookmark my butt.
You too slow and can't run I holler.
I'm running to the end of the world.

I turn the corner
as fast as Omar
can turn a page.

Omar and the Baby Yona

Folks call Omar's mom
Mama Clara.
So she's Mama Clara to me.

I like to peek my head
into the kitchen whenever
I visit Omar's house.

Mama Clara knows so much
she tells me things that make my
school books drop open and listen.

I can't remember everything she says
because she talks fast and slow at the same time
and reminds me of the school light we have

that's always yellow and not green or red.
Only thing you can do is stand there and
listen to Mama Clara.

If it's Saturday you will be standing there
for a long time.
Light be stuck on yellow and you be a fool

to think it's green.
When you're small you better grow ears so the
rest of you can grow.

I'm still taller than Omar but he is catching me
like the wind blowing behind my neck.
That's why I like to stand in the doorway

of Mama Clara's kitchen and feel the warm air
and smells coming out of all those pots and pans.
Mama Clara sure can cook and the stories she tells

just spills out like something good you just
can't get enough of.
It was Mama Clara who one Christmas told

me the story of the Baby Yona.
I had brought a gift for Omar and couldn't find
any Muslim wrapping paper at the drug store.

So I had to wrap it using brown paper and draw
pictures with a magic marker.
TO OMAR, I wrote.

I signed it MJ.
I started doing that after Jordan stopped
playing basketball. MJ

Omar asked me if that stood for me and Jesus.
I said maybe Michael Jordan was God and Omar
knows nothing about basketball or Jesus.

Omar don't even have a TV in his house
but maybe he don't need one with all those
stories Mama Clara tells.

Mama Clara be all the channels.
She be BET and CNN.
Mama Clara be NASA and know how to fill

the space in your head.
You ever heard about the story of the Baby Yona?
she said when she caught me peeking at a pie

she was making.
Omar was in his room saying his prayers
or whatever he has to do all the time.

Omar takes those types of timeouts
you be taking when the game is close or in overtime.
You be doing something and all of a sudden

Omar says he has to pray.
And so it be timeout from whatever we doing.
You ever see MJ take a timeout? I ask Omar

knowing he don't ever see a game.
MJ don't take no timeout
He has all the time in the world.

It be one second left.
Or a second of a second
and MJ still beat you.

Why call timeout and let time mess up your game?
Only reason MJ retired was because he didn't want
time to mess up his game.

Everybody knows that, don't they?
Mama Clara don't call no timeout either.
She just be telling you something and you know

it's time to listen.
So that's how I learned the story
about the Baby Yona.

Folks think it's some kind of African tale
or something that bald headed guy in
California made-up.

Maybe it is African.
Omar's dad said the Baby Yona tale sounded
like something Toni Morrison would write.

I don't know who she is
But I'm keeping my eye out.
Omar's dad said she wrote a book called Paradise.

And I ask him, *Why should she do that?*
Don't she have a
Bible?

The Equator

So what's that line around your nose
the equator or something? I'm in the playground
sitting next to Omar and in between him and Natalie.

She's the new girl
with the old clothes who moved into
the corner house one month ago.

What you talking about? she squeaks.
Her voice has that little girl sound
like she could sing high notes

and maybe call herself Mariah
but she's just Natalie
from down the street.

Why you staring at my nose? You just
a silly looking boy with one of those
mooslem hats on your head.

You shouldn't even be looking at me.
Why should I let you look at me?
Why? You tell me why?

I'm between Omar and Natalie and this
is what my Momma means when she says
If you make your bed you gotta lie in it.

Or maybe this is just a hard place
and the rock is here too.
I don't know.

It was me who decided not to do my homework,
so here I am listening to Omar trying to talk
all smart and talk about geography

like he knows where he is.
Omar don't know nothing about no equator.
You can't see the equator fool! I tell him.

You just want to mess with Natalie's nose.
In between my words, her tears gather like
clouds coming from behind the big buildings

and telling us it's time to go.
But it's Natalie's crying which make me shiver.
She stutters and tries to find her own rain of words.

My daddy broke my nose when I was small
because I didn't stop crying.
He broke my nose and it left a mark.

Natalie's words catch Omar and me like we
were running and now we both out of breath.
Omar pushes me out the way and puts his arm

around Natalie's shoulder like he's the equator.
I guess this was the right thing to do
if we added our ages together.

Sometimes Omar does things I wish I could do.
Sometimes he just sees things
I'm too young to see.

Looking for Omar

I'm in the school bathroom
washing my hands without
soap but I'm still washing my hands.

I turn the water off
and look for a paper towel
but paper towels have been gone
since the first day of school
and it's June now.

I start to leave the bathroom
with my wet hands but then
the big boys come in talking
loud and cussing like they
rap stars or have new sneakers.

I hear the one named Pinto
talking about how someone
should get Omar after school
since he's the only Muslim they know.

Pinto talks with an accent
like he's new in the neighborhood too.

I don't have to ask him
what he's talking about
since everybody is talking
about the Towers and how they
ain't there no more.

My momma said it's like
a woman losing both

breasts to cancer and my daddy
was talking at the dinner table
about how senseless violence is
and Mrs. Gardner next door lost
two tall boys to drive-bys

Bullets flying into
both boys heads
making them crumble too.

Everybody around here is
filled with fear and craziness
and now Pinto and the big boys
thinking about doing something bad.

I stare at my wet hands
dripping water on my shoes
and wonder if I should run
and tell Omar or just run.

I feel like I'm trapped
in the middle of one of those
Bible stories but it ain't
Sunday.

I hear my Momma's voice
saying

Boy, always remember to wash
your hands but always remember
you can't wash your hands from
everything.

Nashville, TN
10/12/01

The Cathedral of Saint Matthew

Under the dome of love
your fingers dip into holy water
I turn to see the light in your eyes

How can I confess how I feel at this moment?
If this is God's house, where is ours?
Come follow me

I will be your disciple forever

Rebecca lets down her hair

I am a victim
of my own war
as I stand in the
shower watching
my hair fall and
swim

Is this worse
than cancer
this loss of
hair?

Why do I
think of balding
men in war
camps and
Japanese
women after
the bomb?

I love
my hair
as much
as life

to brush
to comb
to hold

My hair
no longer
in my eyes

Rebecca hides her scar

The affair
was about finding the rest of me.
There were moments when I wanted
to be the other woman I dressed up to be.

When I was a girl
I loved to walk into my mother's room
open the drawers to her dresser,
search for her secrets.

The affair
was something I could place beneath
the scar on my chest.
I needed fingerprints on my flesh.

I needed someone other than Jim.
Is this a crime?
I wanted desire and not death.
This cancer is deeper than guilt.

Maybe it's me that's growing out of control.
Maybe it's this unspeakable love which kills.

When my lover touches me
it feels like the first time…
My body is new again.
Nothing is broken.
Nothing needs repair.

God
I have no prayers and only one breast.
I call my lover's name, and he answers.

Dreaming about Katherine Dunham

The sound of their voices
against the bedroom door
is like rain falling next
to the face of Lena Horne.

My husband talks to our daughter
about money, bills, insurance
and stormy weather.

Since the accident
I've been knocked down like a
girl in a high school fight.

In the corner of the room
a wheelchair glistens like a chariot.
Who will now turn around to whistle at my legs?

When the name Jesus slips from my lips
I think about the distance to the toilet
and how being able to take a piss by myself
is a step toward heaven.

Bud

Bud Powell plays Bird
Piano flying with notes
Ornithology

In A Silent Way

When we were sick
we were very sick of Lincoln Hospital
where one night a doctor told my mother to take
the scarf off her head so he could tie my broken
wrist and I learned you couldn't fool my
mother by acting a fool even if you were white and had
one of those things around your neck and someone called
you doctor instead of Auntie who is the person I
remember had all the cures for every relative in Brooklyn

We lived in the Bronx and the stores were
filled with boxes of epsom salt and where
it came from no one knew and so
we thought it came from the Nile or Mississippi
or from the place where they caught flying fish
and the accents were like bubbles in our ginger ale

One day my grandfather died and my
mother soaked her feet all day long and my father
thought about taking her to the hospital but she
was not sick just humming to herself in a silent way
a sound I would recognize coming from the horn
of Miles years later in an apartment where my lady
scattered my clothes and books across the room
like salt before she left

New York: St. Vincent's Hospital

At the foot of the bed
I watch Marie and Enid hold your hands,
touching you for the last time.
You are the first person I will see die in a hospital.
Your body warm, your skin smooth and wonderful.
You were always concerned about how you looked,
especially your face. Even now you are handsome.
How funny to see you at peace. You were always in bed
sleeping or watching television. Whenever I came to visit
you were in the bedroom listening to your own heart beat.
Occasionally you would rise and talk with a visitor, but
this was only occasionally. My memories of you are like
tonight. The quietness of death is a predictable conversation.
I can't believe you're my father, that the tubes removed
from your arms were as life giving as your blood. I feel like
a stranger before you. A man left with two women, a
mother and sister. I cannot comfort them. What could one
say that would caress? What words could open your eyes?

14th Street Station

I want to hug you close
in subways that no longer
belong to New York and feel
the softness beneath your
dress like when you walk or
dance and the poetry is in
your eyes and I read them
aloud and taste the words
on my tongue and to speak
another language is to love
and touch you tonight or to
follow you home is to say
I will miss you whenever
I breathe in dark places or
where trains run and your
hands remain invisible on
my chest like tracks we
might one day cross

Barnes & Noble

We pull a copy of
*The Best American
Poetry* from a bookshelf.
Like two college students
on a first date we exchange
the names of jazz musicians
and abstract painters. Does
David Lehman know about
us?

La La La

I stack my old albums
against the wall. The music
of my youth falling out of
covers and sleeves. So many
things are scratched and filled
with memories. I once danced all
night to the Delfonics. I held a
woman close and whispered *La
La La* into her ears. Today my daughter
has those eyes that sing. On the
day she was born I entered a hospital
room and heard her mother humming
"Somebody Loves You Girl" or maybe
it was something just as beautiful.

It Must Be Lester Young

Saturday in August. Marie is down from New York.
I take her to see Nagorka, a psychic on 16th street.
Afterwards we go to the New Orleans Café. We order fried
catfish and Hurricanes. If you sit at one of the two
tables near the window people can see you from outside.
Columbia Road is always busy. Marie talks about Nagorka.
I spot a few friends. It takes longer to find an attractive
girl. It's late afternoon. Around the corner the Sun Gallery
is still open. I hardly go there but since Marie is visiting
I change my mind. She pays for the catfish and drinks. We
leave a nice tip. Four dollars. Our empty glasses stand
side by side like lovers. Much of what I remember
about my sister can be painted on a small canvas. Here we
are at a house party. Marie is in junior high school. I am
eight years old holding a potato chip and a cup of punch. It's
a big night for my sister. Many of her friends are here. This
night is uneventful but will change my life. I discover I
can't dance. The music jumps from the record player splashing
my arms, face and legs. My sister's friends laugh at my
awkward attempts at moving. I try to dance. There is a small
stain on Marie's dress. I notice this as we walk down 18th Street.
We pass three Ethiopian restaurants and someone who is majoring
in business at Howard. Inside the Sun Gallery we look at prints
made by Honeywood. I pick-up a post-card of a famous jazz
musician. It must be Lester Young.

My House

In my house my son slips
his arms into my shirt and
stretches to see if it fits.

I can remember when I wore
my father's shoes around my
house. My small feet swirling

inside his black wingtips.
A tall silence now embraces me
as my son walks out my house.

His pants need a belt and his
head a hat. The front door to
my house closes with my echo.

Birds

I don't count birds
so when the fourth body hits the floor
I stop counting because it's too easy
shooting people with a gun and besides
I forgot my math book and where it is
is anybody's guess including my own

My daddy placed this gun in my hand
when I was crawling after things crawling
Rabbits
Squirrels
Cats
Dogs
Who cares if they have four legs or two

I just like to aim and shoot and taste the
rush it gives me like the roller coaster
at the fair and the cotton candy and root
beer and the hot dogs and pickles and relish
dripping down the side of my hands

Red spot in my eye but I keep shooting
teachers and kids until the gun clicks
and the fun runs out and I know this
must be the movies because I'm alive
and everyone else is dead

In Shadows There Are Men

We were never absent
or invisible
we were always here

Our lives interrupted
by what others
wanted to see

Sometimes what
we want is the
taste of the kiss
and the touch of
a hand

Even our women
stare at us
disgusted with how
we live

Never knowing
how we struggle
to love

All that could go wrong

now fills my life.
The face of my father
is now my own.

My hands now show
their age and not what
they have built.

I cannot sit at the
kitchen table without
thinking of him.

Head bent over his
meal and feeling the
heat of it against his brow.

How hungry I was to know
what he felt and how afraid
of my father's hunger I became.

A man in my own house
with my wife's back to me.
In bed where I might have

slept alone if it was not
for some sense of duty
to death or marriage or

whatever comes next in this
life which kills so slowly
and every breath is his breath.

12/31/01

Geography

My four year old daughter comes home
from school with a map of the world. This
is Africa she tells me. This is where we
come from. Daddy watch me color the rest
of the world. I watch her color Europe red
and all of the Atlantic. I try to encourage
the use of blues and greens but she refuses.
She sees the world with her own brown eyes.
My daughter stops coloring and prints her
name at the top of her map. Jasmine, she
says like a young Columbus. Her mouth
round with wonder.

Midnight Caller

What could I do?
The boy was a man so soon,
so suddenly outgrowing his clothes,
his arms, his room,
my love.
What could I do
but close the door,
knowing not even God or hymn or prayer
could bring him back or make him be a boy again.
My son, a child, so tender, soft and dear.
A boy, a man, he thought he was tonight.
Tonight he killed a man.

Tonight
I heard my telephone ring.
I picked it up.
I knew the news was bad.
I did not wait to hear.
I knew tonight.
Tonight I knew.
Tonight he killed a man.

Fishing

She laid half on, half off the bed, crying and begging
for her mom. Her hair spread like broken wings and fallen
feathers, as if the night had lost its way. John searched
for a light, so I took my cigarette and passed it to his
mouth. My hand steady because I have no man to fear. The girl
moaning, sweating, panting; her face scarred, her legs
branded by what we spilled. I could feel her watching the smoke
curl in front of John's eyes. I knew she wanted to cover her
face and the many places from where she bled. John spoke
first because I never have much to say.

He talked with the cigarette hanging from his lips
and with a second breath he said, the best ever, the best
I ever had. The best he swore. The best I nodded and agreed.
Unaware of what drove me here. What rage forced me to this
room? What anger came from deep inside where folks blame
John and my daddy who disappeared? I confess it was not
pleasure that I felt or pleasure that I took and what I did
I've done before.   Like fishing.

67

Liberia Fever, 1877

My youngest comes running
out of the summer nightmare
chased by white men who would
prefer us dead instead of free

When I sleep the same dream
returns like a ship sailing across water
sweating I toss in my bed while my wife
mumbles a prayer for protection

All our possessions
in our hands
We walk on the same land that planted
scars on our backs and feet

Many folks suffer from a strange fever
Something cured only by the touch of an African
wind

Anna Murray Douglass

I cannot read the North Star
but it shines at night in my bedroom.
I hold a free man in my arms.
Is it love that still keeps me a slave?
What speech could he whisper in my ears
that would make me listen to his heart?
In the dark does my dark skin remind him
of the darkness?
I cannot spell the word abolitionist.
I can only read the name Frederick Douglass.
I know these two words well.
Many will remember the life he lived.
And me? Yes, they will say I was his wife
before he married the white woman.

Nothing But A Man

When he turns to sleep on his side
I stare at his back and place my hand
where segregation once was.

If my lover is the black messiah
then tonight I rest his crown on my head.

Martin—I whisper in the dark.
Our presence in this hotel room
is like a candle ready to be knocked over.

Fire spreading like love.
Rumors leaping to a tape recorder
next door.

8/6/01

Crosetti

Frank Crosetti
a gentleman in pinstripes
stands near third base.

How many heroes
will he escort home?

1932 and Ruth looks into
the Cubs dugout,
points a finger and calls
the shot.

A young Crosetti will think
of the Babe when he shakes
the hand of Roger Maris in
1961.

Baseball is a game played
by men who know the silence
of grace and the beauty of
records made to be broken

A Poem For Richard

At two and three in the morning
when sleep walks away like a lover

I think of Richard Wright
Dead at fifty-two

He lived in a small apartment in France
alone without Ellen or the kids

A few days before Wright died
Langston Hughes knocked on his door

Here was the poet of Harlem
saying hello to the black boy and native son

I think about Langston looking
into Richard's eyes and searching for a river

Maybe the Mississippi moving one more day
down the delta with the blues

Alexander Calder
(1898-1976)

I can make
the world move

Bend
Spin
Flutter

Wind kissing wire
Red metal tickling

Air

4/1/98

E. ETHELBERT MILLER was born in New York City, New York, in 1950. He received his B.A. from Howard University. His poetry collections include *Buddha Weeping in Winter* (2001), *Whispers, Secrets, and Promises* (1998), *First Light: New and Selected Poems* (1994), *Where Are the Love Poems for Dictators?* (1986), *Season of Hunger/Cry of Rain: Poems 1975-1980* (1982), *The Migrant Worker* (1978), and *Andromeda* (1974). He also is editor of many anthologies, including the highly acclaimed *In Search of Color Everywhere: A Collection of African American Poetry* (1994) and *Women Surviving Massacres and Men* (1977). Most recently, he is the author of the memoir *Fathering Words: The Making of an African American Writer* (2000). His awards include the Columbia Merit Award and the O.B. Hardison Jr. Poetry Prize. In 1979, the Mayor of Washington, DC, proclaimed September 28, 1979 as "E. Ethelbert Miller Day." Miller is the director of the African American Resource Center at Howard University, a position he has held since 1974.

CURBSTONE PRESS, INC.

is a non-profit publishing house dedicated to literature that reflects a
commitment to social change, with an emphasis on contemporary writing
from Latino, Latin American and Vietnamese cultures. Curbstone presents
writers who give voice to the unheard in a language that goes beyond
denunciation to celebrate, honor and teach. Curbstone builds bridges
between its writers and the public – from inner-city to rural areas, colleges
to community centers, children to adults. Curbstone seeks out the highest
aesthetic expression of the dedication to human rights and intercultural
understanding: poetry, testimonies, novels, stories,
and children's books.

This mission requires more than just producing books. It requires ensuring
that as many people as possible learn about these books and read them. To
achieve this, a large portion of Curbstone's schedule is dedicated to
arranging tours and programs for its authors, working with public school
and university teachers to enrich curricula, reaching out to underserved
audiences by donating books and conducting readings and community
programs, and promoting discussion in the media. It is only through these
combined efforts that literature can truly make a difference.

Curbstone Press, like all non-profit presses, depends on the support of
individuals, foundations, and government agencies to bring you, the reader,
works of literary merit and social significance which might not find a place
in profit-driven publishing channels, and to bring the authors and their
books into communities across the country. Our sincere thanks to the many
individuals, foundations, and government agencies who have recently
supported this endeavor: Connecticut Commission on the Arts, Connecticut
Humanities Council, Fisher Foundation, Greater Hartford Arts Council,
Hartford Courant Foundation, J. M. Kaplan Fund, Lannan Foundation, John
D. and Catherine T. MacArthur Foundation, National Endowment for the
Arts, Open Society Institute, Puffin Foundation, and the Woodrow Wilson
National Fellowship Foundation.

Please help to support Curbstone's efforts to present the diverse voices and
views that make our culture richer. Tax-deductible donations can be made by
check or credit card to:
Curbstone Press, 321 Jackson Street, Willimantic, CT 06226
phone: (860) 423-5110   fax: (860) 423-9242
www.curbstone.org

IF YOU WOULD LIKE TO BE A MAJOR SPONSOR OF A
CURBSTONE BOOK, PLEASE CONTACT US.